T0096443

# Blood Rain

*For Ros, always*
*and to Michael Bayley, with gratitude*


*The sun shall be turned to darkness, and the moon to blood.*
*– Joel 2:31*

# Blood Rain

*André Mangeot*

Seren is the book imprint of
Poetry Wales Press Ltd.
57 Nolton Street, Bridgend, Wales, CF31 3AE
www.serenbooks.com
facebook.com/SerenBooks
twitter@SerenBooks

ISBN: 978-1-78172-562-7
ebook: 978-1-78172-563-4

A CIP record for this title is available from the British Library.

The publisher acknowledges the financial assistance of the Welsh Books Council.

Cover photograph: Every effort has been made to trace copyright ownership of the
cover photo. The publisher welcomes any information that enables it to include due
acknowledgement in subsequent printings.

Author photograph: Sarah K. Hall

Printed in Bembo by Bell & Bain Ltd, Glasgow.

# Contents

*Soon silence will have passed into legend.*
— Jean Arp

# Oxbow

Remember, too, our secret pool? How in those burning
weeks the river turned its back and took another path,
leaving us to stumble on that slow and curved meander,

a perfect O? Screened by rushes in the glow of evening
only we, its first explorers, appeared to know the truth
about that sacred circle where, with bestial hunger

we came to know each other, the sky alone approving.
But ever since, and just as true, it seems we've both
assumed life's yoke, tugging us with unseen pressure

at another's whim, down furrows darkening, unfurling
at our backs like clods of earth. Now it's but the breath
of memory, and something else, across our shoulders.

# Bellwether

At first it was nothing – a thought, a cough in a gale
then just a voice, then another, till none could be heard
but all spoke as one. And some called it chatter
and some called it rumour. And soon came a leader

who cut through the babble to what we were saying,
told us why and to who, and now we were more
than the sum of ourselves. Some called it bigotry,
others theology. On you led till nothing could

touch us, till each glance we caught looked away
and no challenge came. Loyal to a fault we pressed on
in your wake. To some a messiah, to the rest a base liar,
we were all on a bandwagon now and – hazard or bluff,

right to the brink – some called it hate, some called it love.

# Wild Honey

Twisting the spoon in deep, you watch gold uncoil
into your porridge bowl where bees and butterflies
are lacquered round the rim. Beyond the glass
it's several summers since they buzzed and flitted
through our thistle-spotted grass, the back-meadow's
poppy, yarrow, lady's bedstraw. From even there
mites and parasites – varroa, wax moth, foulbrood –
have thinned them to a smatter and now with diggers,
ploughs and cutters three hedgerows in a day and
every flower goes under – another swathe of pasture
laid out for its bypass. And so, watched only by
the stars, pockets bursting, we steal out and scatter
through the night, packet after packet: red campion,
crested dogstail, birdsfoot trefoil, viper's bugloss.

# Heart

Impatient, our first afternoon
we boot straight up, waterproofs and rucksack

strike out through the mizzle, up from
Parkergate along the ridge of Ullock Pike –

stickleback of false and teasing summits.
Skin chilling as the cloud-mist settles,

weaves and licks around the map, the dotted track
we hold but cannot see – Dodd Wood, the conifers

below to lead us down and back. So on we go,
higher, higher till it's madness – too high, too far –

you're finished, hands on knees then braced
against the rock before you straighten, gasp *don't worry*

*it's ok, just my...heart murmur*, and we stand there
whipped by rain, staring blankly like two lunatics.

*Christ*, I say, *great time and place to mention it* –
dissolving suddenly together into aching laughter

and now my own heart's racing too, swept and
blown between these streaming moments, skin numb,

rivulets for faces, alone and lost to everyone
but one another – helpless, weeping on the mountain –

and you there in your rattling hood, brim-full of it.

# Helvellyn

What is it, this need to rise,
to climb, to go clear
of the track, of signpost
and small-talk,
swallowed by scale?

Why suffer this burning
of muscle and lung,
wind-chill and no-looking-down
along Striding Edge? Here we are,
scrabbling through shale for the top –

less to high-circling ravens
than chaff in the gale,
gaps in a drystone wall,
that sheep's skull
picked clean in the beck.

# Uhtceare

*Lying in bed I wonder, 'When will day come?'* — Job 7:4

Awake in the pre-dawn,
hijacked from sleep by the babble
and dart of worries,
draw comfort from this:

we are never alone.

Everywhere now, others
stare into dark, partners in dread
confusion, despair —
we're hardwired to wonder

what is this torment?

And with Job, Chaucer, Cuthbert
in his Lindisfarne cell —
fellow first-lighters of candle
and lamp, pacing the still-silent hours —

to be blessed with a word for it.

## Opening the Blinds

As every dream unmasks
some predetermined hope, anxiety,
dread — so too each morning.

Rain is never cold or warm, the sun
neither killer nor lover
without us.

The folded shadow we leave
still breathing in that other place
merely a stranger

without these blurry horizons
we share, a history we cannot
recapture, already dissolving,

this cruel glimpse of happiness we call,
for reasons no more explicable, love.

# Encounter

The doe freezes, as do I
and we face one another:
eyes locked, twenty yards apart
holding our ground.

It's 7am. Perfectly still.
Deep in the valley we both
assumed quiet vigils –
lone runner, undisturbed forager.

Now, hemmed in by the tunnel-like
thicket there is no escape
save past or through the other.
Unblinking, I can read

the thud of your heart, you mine:
duellists tensed for the first
muscle twitch, waiting
for the kerchief to fall.

Then, before I can stir, you're
past me – tawny blur and thump,
a last wild-eyed glance,
close enough to catch the heat

of your flank, heady musk of
your breath. Even running on
my heart's still rooted there,
touched with longing, strange regret.

# Memory

Mounting the cliff-path, nothing prepared us
for that riotous palette: purpled ling- and bell-
heather, blazes of gorse. Callow lovers,

we stood there aghast and speak of them still,
those fast-shrinking heathlands rarer than
rainforest now. Nightjar and stonechat,

do you court there as we did? Sand lizard,
adder, do you bask in our place? Even we,
just twenty years back, gathered bilberries

wild mushroom, watched jade-vivid beetles
dart amid harebell and orchid. And what of
the slow-worm and woodlark, golden-ringed

dragonfly? Has the last copper butterfly
danced away from a bracken-choked ridge
seeking one final smidgen of heath?

# Hawk

*(St Hywyn's Church, Aberdaron)*

After the poem-board at the back, your books
and an honesty-box tucked in an echoey corner
we returned to the wind, clambering the steep
and tussocky slope amid salt-weathered stones
in search of your grave, old hawk. But like you –
self-confessed loner and misanthrope, your stark
metaphysical lines steely as this sweep of sea,
rocky headland – all it revealed was mystery,
presence in absence where storm-gusts, a silent
but beady kestrel, buffet and circle your parish.

# The Counterpoise

Eagles sucked into the turbine blades at Smøla.

Feathers riffling with a memory of breath.

*The most primitive men are the least warlike.*
*Warlikeness grows in proportion to civilization.*
— Eric Fromm

# Foot & Mouth

And once the pyres were lit the starless lanes and fields
soon flared with beacons, for days a sickly smoke
rolled widdershins along the valley, leaching into
every cranny of our rooms, our nostrils till despair

assembled us to troop, whole villages, up to the widow's
homestead where, for recompense, she showed us how to seal
each draughty nook, season coals with white sage, lybcorn,
rosemary, chant runes against such glaring portents:

stench of sulphur, burning flesh, the cloven hoof.

# Blood Rain

Then, hazing the horizon, silting lungs, it came
by night, silent and unseen, this dust-shroud
blown and shed like desiccated blood –
laid upon our cars, our streets as if in admonition
from a wounded continent, an augury of rust.

Science, meteorology – the latest prophets
grapple to agree on composition, colour,
this copper-tinged phenomena:
algae, desert sand, unknown spores
sucked northward in their churning centrifuge.

And yet, be certain what it promises, such rain,
and what they hold for us, these winds from Africa.

# Scrimshaw

Only there, watchmaker's son, hollowed out
by all you have seen, by trench-foot and rain,
by shell-thunder's undying, murderous hail

only then do you scavenge for tools with your
artisan chums, improvise metal-punch, scriber,
discover his artistry's passed to your hands.

Moon- and frost-lit, lulls are the eeriest: numb
in the foxhole's flicker and stink, you hammer
and craft jags of shrapnel, bayonets, bullets

into match-boxes, lighters, this cigarette-case
that in fear of an officer's wrath (weapons and
ordnance are government property) you inscribe

with a wry *nom de guerre*, a nod to your maritime
brothers – scrimshoner-sailors, carvers of whale-tooth
and bone. Then, whoever you were, you vanish

'Jack Scrimshaw', outside Le Cateau: flung from
your mates by the splintering air, blown and sunk
like your brass baccy case into rubble and mud,

sword into ploughshare. But here, a hundred years
later – agleam, resurrected – is Lot 41, *unrivalled
example of trench-art*, waiting again on the hammer.

# The Gift

Sure – tinsel, ribbons, wrapping
but a gift
can be many things:

motivating teacher, lifeguard's grasp,
just a voice on the line.

Man is defined by his choices.

Across seventy years it's still spring
near a small Austrian village. A fine April morning,
warm breeze through the wire, as the first
of three hundred men, young Soviets,
drops to the ground.

Every two minutes, the same:

a single shot at close range, no bullet wasted,
one further prisoner, another, another –
through the dusk they're still falling
till the last youth crumples, lies still,
and the Kommandant salutes, turns on his heel.

And that night his wife's back is warm, life
surges through him, knowing outside –
silver-wrapped by a moon
for the Führer's birthday – his gift.

# Lost at Cadiz

The last time then, edging with a tray into your dark:
the bed and chair, this cell your voyaging has come to.
Bread, porridge, tea – same condemned man's breakfast
every day – for how long now? Two years? Three?
And now it's D-Day for us both. *Hello Ted –*
letting in the useless light. *Manage any sleep?*
I set the pillows, ease you up, your navigator's eyes
still bloodshot, cloudy, struggling for a fix on me.

More night-time wounds. Table, lampstand overturned.
Scab and scar and bruise – a brow-cut, fresh. *Back in
combat, eh?* (Groping, compass haywire through
the foggy hours, floor rolling like Atlantic swell,
you're undermined by neurons now.) *Aye... you hear
that thunder, son? Flashes like them guns again...
fair shook the bed.* Tea pitching in the mug, you wash
the tablets down – though even when the trembling calms

you won't be sailing far, not once sickness, lethargy
kick in – wave on wave of Sinemet and Madopar.
The tuning on the radio's slipped: the shipping news
arrives, recedes. I flush the dregs of night away;
lay out fresh clothes; steer you, groggy, to a basin
where you fasten on the taps (your gunwale, haven)
while the water runs. The discipline's sustained us
for this long – but though I'm ready for tomorrow

(new job, new town, the moving on) today we know
its other purpose. Recall together, as you dress,
the first time that I searched in vain (and then your
explanation, still unchanged) for that elusive vest.
*Lord no, you'll not find that! Las' one I 'ad
were on that same damn sweeper. Shot to hell
it was. Torpedoes... bombs. This'd be – by 'eck,
let's think – forty-two or three, sumwheres off Cadiz...*

sinking finally into your chair. *Right raw today,*
*or is it me?* I find the rug, fit it snug around your knees
then softly back toward the door – determined to escape
an exit-line. But you've seen it coming. Seen through me.
*Go careful, son. Don't be minding…I'll be grand.* Your stare
consumes the shadow where I stand. *Goodbye Ted–*
*be good. And no more wandering alone.* I close the door,
seeing still your eyes – and all their broken, burning vessels.

# Blood

The way Calea Victoriei twists and meanders, a somnolent python
past *fin de siècle* railings, libraries of dust, The Red Palace
strip-joint then all of a sudden
uncoils in a yawn on this wasteland of menace,

Piața Revoluției, Revolution Square
where our gaze is drawn, but of course,
to the lofty veranda where
one little man, the Creed-Shaper, Danube of Thought, waved first to
applause…

it calls into mind, from no clear or good reason,
what your flush-with-pride niece, raising
high her first-born from its cushions
at the post-christening

bash, confided from nowhere, still cradling her Merlot
…*but so unprepared! – Did you know that the cord*
*isn't snipped or tied in a neat little knot, no*
*the stub is still there till it drops of its own sweet accord*

*and Lord does it stink in the meantime, seep something rotten,*
*much the same colour*…with a swirl of the wine –
details I'd all but forgotten
till we came on this supplicant hand, this statue of Cain

like a last frozen witness in the now-blameless present,
eyes trained like our own, past a scatter of tourists,
on the same granite terrace
as we read on his back in Romanian and English

*What hast thou done? The sound,*
*the voice of thy brother's blood*
*crieth unto me from the ground*
and, glancing up, the same little man might have stood

there again, no more than a dot
on that morning, just before Christmas,
in overcoat, scarf, absurd little hat –
Nimbus of Victory, Wise Helmsman, Carpathian Genius

waving first at the press–ganged applause
then, as each mike and camera
exposed, through an upsurge of catcalls and boos,
to the chant *Ti-mi-şoa-ra! Ti-mi-şoa-ra!*

*We are the people! Romania awake!*
till tear-gas hovered and hissed
and the gunfire popped and the little man waved
and hey presto – like the day, like its people – he vanished.

# The Odds

Stall to stall, a child in Delhi runs
his barefoot errands: tea-trays, lemons, bolts of cloth.
In northern Chad, a mud-walled mosque
is shelter from the scarring sand as boyhood friends
bow down in prayer. Somewhere in London an alarm-clock fails
to bring the student-medic to her ward-round
while a teacher rides the A-train back downtown
from Harlem, his book-filled rucksack lined with Semtex, nails.

It's said we've more in common than divides us.
Can something be both false and true? The younger ones will come
to what they know by imitation or disdain, not reason,
and there are secrets stored in any heart or house.
Clutching his rupees, the Indian child runs
back across the street, light as air, his only god the sun.

# Jerusalem

The laughter from the café barely touches him,
sidewalk drinkers looking skyward as the sun goes in.
Heaven's road is paved with selflessness and sin.

Walking on, he thinks of Lena and the twins.
A twinge of longing gnaws away within
but the laughter from the café barely touches him.

It's all down now to faith, to faith and discipline;
a homeland, freedom…justice in Jerusalem.
Heaven's road is paved with selflessness and sin.

Across his path stroll women, children, men.
His head's a minaret, his inner voice the muezzin.
Laughter from the café barely touches him.

Entering the bar, sweat's cooling on his skin.
In *yarmulkah* and tassels no one's noticing.
Heaven's road is paved with selflessness and sin.

A waiter hurries by him bearing drinks.
Their eyes meet briefly in the mirror as he pulls the pin.
The laughter from the café barely touches him.
Heaven's road is paved with selflessness and sin.

# Depth Charge

*(for Adam McGuiness)*

Out of the war's dark waves, submariner
did you surface breathing bubbles of relief
or find the sudden overload of space and light
too much? Just once, out on the loch
you spoke of that mortal co-dependence,
death's ever-present hum, its edge. Is that why
you couldn't settle, wandered from coast
to hinterland and back, from one tight confine
to another – North Sea rigger, caver, undertaker?
Now, silenced by the stroke, you signal me
to tap out your tablets. Here they sit, pillboxes
next to your chair: little white drums,
each one a depth-charge, primed for attack.

# Cognac

The Beetle sputters smokily across the square
bumping over cobbles, an umber dusk already
heady with intoxicant. Day ten of your tour
of wartime comrades, those who remain,

and here is Jacques, another veteran gnarly
as an olive tree, bending to the window,
pointing to the open gates beside the factory,
*Le Manoir*, wreathed in autumn creeper.

*"Bienvenue, amis!"* Parked up, he leads us
straight to the distillery – his joy, his life.
"Alain, my son, will show you round. He owns
the secrets now. *Mais, prenez garde:* his wife

is not so good, now the baby's near."
Already stooped and pale from years in cellars
Alain guides us through the looming stills
and down to catacombs where gravid barrels

seep burnt scent. Uncorking one, he blows
just gently: the hit's immediate, right behind
the eyes. We taste, spit, savour and compare.
It's then, emerging, that the message comes.

A pause, a breath, a father's hand upon his arm.
We have no words. He bows, his grip is firm.
*"This work too"*, he sighs, *"is patience. Time and God.
With His blessing, we will make another one."*

## Paradise

Listen, where are you going with this?

With your vapid slogans of rage
hideous death-cult
sneering psychopathy?

Show us your paradise, chapter and verse –
what's left once you're done,
how it's worth it.

Look, here is *jannah*
right under your nose

down among the rock-pools
where the water's still clear,
where the child dips her spade in
and stirs. Explores with her fingers
green slippy stones,
tiny swimmers, skittering claws.

See, this is everything
worthy of heaven,
a present worth having,
a future to fight for

not some phantom invention
whose only motive is hatred
whose only mantra is murder
whose only lover is death.

# The Puppeteer

– ashen, sweating, grasps the lectern; trots out an auto-cue apology,
self-justifies.

Placards, chants demand atonement. Far off, another shopping-centre's
vaporised.

*My family is my strength, and my weakness.*
— Aishwarya Rai

## Pommade divine

You gave the room its calm, its warmth
a landing door that opened

onto sunlight, gauzy curtains billowing,
quilted diamonds vibrant on your bed

and scents impressed so deep that even now
I could be breathing in your Nivea-ed skin

kissing both your cheeks to catch
the dabbed cologne, the apple-sweet *pommade*

that lent your hair (drawn back beneath
the soft felt band) its lustrous grey-black sheen.

&#9733;    &#9733;    &#9733;

We'd unfold the frayed old board,
set out magic figurines, rival knights

and bishops, rooks and kings, and patiently
you'd show me how they slid and schemed

among their chequered paving-stones
while these almost-secret moments –

a sense of perfect safety – led my
wriggling inattention to your face's

lined and olive beauty, bent in concentration:
how light glinted from your glasses

and always to the curtained cubbyhole
(your dressing-room) where I'd glimpse

that ancient strongbox, surely packed with
pirate's booty, which no one saw you open.

&#9733;    &#9733;    &#9733;

Only later, turning your room into mine,
would I plunge my hands into a sea of letters

drifts of air-mail, eighty years of postmarks,
waxy carbons: your life, and still your scent.

# Four Dogs

Skylarks, salty breeze across the dunes
and you there on the practice field,
absorbed. Pitching, driving balls
while behind your back another
ball of white, down-soft, slips your mind,
her lead, and starts its sniffing zig-zag
wander in the wrong direction.

I often think it started then – from when,
back home, you tried but failed to tell us
why you'd taken her, the one we doted on
and you had never walked or shown
the merest interest in. From there the snarling
stand-off of our teenage years began,
circling, growling round that buried knot

of blame, the unsolved definitions
of *an accident; forgiveness*. Father, son:
each of us is locked in certain roles.
You and I, in any case, could not move on,
snapped and bit ostensibly on other grounds
until we had forgotten who we were,
what, if any, was the bond between us.

Never fully reconciled, just older beasts
observing an uneasy truce, it wasn't long
before the end that you confessed – the night
you lost her, another dog appeared. Disguised
as solace, it clambered over you for weeks,
a huge black hound; then nightly laid its weight
across your sleeping face, as if to smother you.

# History

Back home, at a loss
we sift on in silence,
pull one more shoebox
from under your bed

and holding this card
I can hear you again,
seem right at your side
as I never was then –

'67, the Airshow,
Le Bourget rotunda,
thunderous flypasts
hubbub of lunch

a stir round your table
as the cosmonaut passed –
inking this scrap
you carried home safe –

something we shared,
something like love
those few magic weeks
while it lit up my face

hour upon hour
simply tracing his name
almost touching the flame
in this one word

*Gagarin*

still floating,
now fading,
around it
just space.

# Ash

Mornings like this, before the haze lifted
you'd have swum with the sunrise, breakfasted well,
been first even then to the boatyard, pushing off
your Loch Long from the slipway, carried out
past the anchored patricians, through Tempests and Dragons,
their tap-tapping halyards applauding your gliding,
that water-slap salt-muddy tang as your featherlight cradle
tacked by in a flapping of canvas, set its downriver course
for Blackstakes and Orford and sight of the sea, surrendered
to gusts that tugged at your dandelion wisps, your brick-red
windbreaker cheeks that beamed in that solitary bliss

and again now you drift
from my grasp, sift from the clench of my palm
in this cool early mist to re-enter the shallows,
the last pale semblance of you, shimmering afloat
on the slipway, light as blown dandelion still, at play
like a shoal clinging yet to itself, still somehow
a body, this albescent glow moving under the surface,
shining back its own ghost-light, some mysterious
new being settling into your element, pausing
here in the lap of clear water –
luminous, swaying, slowly deeper and out –
weightless, ashimmer, released.

# Birdcalls

Surely they were there
at the appointed hour
outside that thrumming London mall

chirruping somewhere
in the haze-blue ether
above those market stalls

invisible and undetected
opposite the Underground
in burnished August –

celestial chatter on the boughs
and trunks of aerials, 3G masts,
the sing-song wires their branches?

Yet all I heard –
glimpsing you at once,
your dazzling plumage clear

across the intersection's steel-bright river –
was a trader's throaty cry
*taiters, taiters….pound a bag*

then, fording counter-current
to a shriek of recognition,
your lilting Trini call –

some east-blown Manakin
or Jacamar that spoke my name
as if from Guanapo or Maraval.

But surely it was there –
that other celebratory chorus
trilling ceaselessly

above, beyond us
along with all, so blinkered now,
we neither heard nor noticed?

# Sunburn

300 feet above the castle keep
500 higher
than the 40 miles of Irish Sea
becalmed with glitter
held between these wide-spread arms

today we've climbed and clung
with ragged sheep
on 1-in-3's of straggling walls
and gorsy paths to reach
Garth Bach –

this dizzy ledge halfway to heaven

swaying breathless
in an ocean light that sweeps
from Bardsey Sound to Barmouth
and beyond

a sheen so bright
it's hard to fathom such a view
or see how castle, beach and bay
don't simply drop away like milk-blue
spindrift into space.

We've come from way down there –
rock-pools to remind us
of all those small and madder leaps
we fear must pass like this day's brilliance –

wind and light that only now I see
suffused in you, so burnt into your skin
you'll carry always from this hill
the hours when

just by stretching out our arms

we seemed to hold the world,
to touch the sun.

# Cromwell

The office clock says 2:16.
Just below it
            on the tessellated screen
the network's locked at
                        2:21.


Where are the missing five minutes?
Are we living within
            or beyond them?


Does this explain
why today our password's
*unrecognised*, our functions *in error*,
why settings just vanish
and the God we call Server
keeps crashing?


Marooned without work
we push back from our keyboards
            peer from small mullioned windows
at the foggy Great Ouse –


we're adrift in a creaking of timbers
            some forgotten wherry or lighter
floating through
                  parallel time.


Look! – clean as vapour
            past Cromwell's old bridge,
its miniature chapel –
                        rising through grapeshot
and gunsmoke, swirl of pennants
                        agonised cries


on we glide
            solitary      silent      untouched
                  noses pressed to the glass
                              phones to our ears

ten thousand Royalists and Roundheads
frozen mid-battle beneath us

blood-lust       terror       despair
fading to wonder
        on their upturned
                petal-pale
      faces.

# Icehouse

*(Ralph Allen 1693–1764)*

In the open-air café our glasses are fizzing with lemonade,
our heads with history. Just imagine, you say, marking
your guide-book, and we squint into glare till lake-dazzle
whitens to ice and Postmaster Allen's first gardeners
and woodsmen, their calls faint and cloudy, emerge
in the snowscape, laden with grapple-hooks, axes,
hauling sledges and carts. Below the Palladian bridge
they saw and heave their cold harvest inshore, up to
its dark winter sepulchre. Slab upon glistening slab
lowered and packed into sackcloth, layers of straw.
Behold wealth! Clear and chill as his hilltop statement
in stone: *built to see all of Bath, for all Bath to see.*
Downing our drinks we climb back toward it, out into
sun-melt, tongue and lips numb from slivers of ice.

# Magpie

*pica* n. Pathol. *an abnormal craving to ingest*
*substances such as clay, dirt or hair, sometimes*
*occurring during pregnancy, in persons with*
*chlorosis etc. [from Latin:* pica pica/*magpie,*
*an allusion to its omnivorous feeding habits]*

Just there, through the glass, they assemble –
oily as teddy-boys, carrion-smug, full of chatter
and swagger. Watching, I even attain a measure
of distance, recalling what peacefulness was

before, in a breath, you're behind me
tugging my hair, screeching with laughter
dashing out, slamming doors, thudding off
up the stairs before I can turn.

Now in the study, searching for *pi*'s
definition, I stumble on *pica*
like providence – key at last to these
latest strange episodes, the still-secret you:

red-handed, 4:00am in the kitchen,
cross-legged in your black-and-white
Toon Army strip by the yawn of the fridge –
pots of cream, frozen sausages, hand-soap

all of it gone, and you, little scavenger,
chuckling, unfazed, irrepressible –
somehow never the worse. Hopping
between us. Flying off through our hands.

# Torrent

*(Lwybr Clywedog, Dolgellau)*

As we walk from the car, drop down from the road
to a canopied path, it begins
as an absence, an aside

somewhere deep in the leaf-light,
drawing us on
down the garlic-thick trail

past chanterelle-gatherers combing
the wood-damp, sifting
earth-orange fungae, on down

to a stile as the murmur expands
opens out
through an over-arched gate to this

torrent of sound, foaming white lung
of the gorge as it sweeps
by the millhouse and under the bridge

we move onto now, where I focus
the lens on the glory of you –
nimbus of light against moss-covered

boulders, spray-mist behind you,
watery rainbow
spanning your shoulders –

blinking the shutter just as you
turn, blurred with the instant
a kingfisher lands

then lower the camera and stare at it
dumbly - gleaming with artifice,
dead in my hands.

# Cuba

Remember that night, just before the main act appeared
at the Stephen Talkhouse, Miami Beach, maybe twenty years back –
you must have known that beret would draw someone to you,
wide-eyed, late arrival, cute curls bobbing
in search of a seat – his glance from the bar intersecting
with yours;

remember the drive back together –
out across Venice Causeway in your beat-up Datsun,
smothering dark, reefer and windrush like static between you –
back to incense and oil, *Steely Dan*,
curtains afloat to the jitter of halyards,
their frantic *a cappella* right under that window;

remember your need, how urgent and brutal
and the subsequent weeks – you the flaky masseuse
zipping round town, three years clean, still making your weekly AA;
him at Bay Shore, would-be pro golfer, slogging balls into heat-haze –
you were each as addicted, both in need of deliverance,

that's why you took off, skipped down the necklace of islands
as far as you could – Key Largo, Key West –
wandered Hemingway's house, asked that woman
to shoot you together by the water-edge buoy as you pointed to Cuba;

remember, in the end
how you knew it had run its brief course,
how you parted
with your eyes, with no more than the instinct
that brought you together,
no longer caring or even remembering
who rescued who.

# Passion

Alone in a cottage on Sark she worked on the novel
disturbed only by gull shrieks, the bleat of new lambs
on the headland. She had a friend's favour to thank –

a Quaker historian at one time her lover, now based
for a year in her place on Anglesey. Still her mentor
if ever more reclusive, concluding his own life's plan.

They shared a passion for islands, synagogues, mosques
and the writings of Marxist theologians.  Her book
was narrated by one, Ernesto Cardenal, the renowned

Nicaraguan priest-poet rebuked by John Paul II. Three men
in all, of landlocked beginnings. Who'd longed to escape,
to end their days in just such a spot as she occupied now –

staring out to sea, creating claustrophobic cities,
jungles that advanced word by word like colony ants,
like implacable foot-soldiers across the blank page.

# The Fabulists

Embarking, we are always dreamers. Odysseus
distracted all those years from Troy to Ithaca,
Dante's, Conrad's passage to the heart of darkness,
James T. Kirk advancing boldly on the future.
Now you and I upon *Minerva's* fore-deck, Chatwin
and Eberhardt perhaps, each eyeing the horizon
for our personal grail as we edge out from Valetta.
Tonight an eminent professor's due to talk on *Honour*
*as a leitmotif in Ancient Greece*, we have no better
guides to point the way, to bring all visible phenomena,
the voyage we shall make, to life. Nonetheless,
what journey, ever, failed to prove a deeper quest?
Embracing self-discovery, my love – hero or villain –
from here we are alone, our own Mercator and Magellan.

# Euston Road

And then, around a corner
you, unmistakably, father
are swept towards me in the human river
wedged so tight in the advancing crowd
it seems to hold you up,
propel you forward

my gaping mouth and tongue
struck dumb upon your name,
a smile unlike any we had shared
in life now lighting you within
as, seeing or unseeing,
you pass right through me.

# A Rosary

Our father, with a convert's conviction you put us to shame.

Blessed mother, to you we entrust these Luminous Mysteries.
Fire warms us, we eat, while news is but horror on horror.
Mouthing Latin, the altar-boy trusted yet understood nothing.
Little light, holy sacrament, guide us from Station to Station.
Coral fades. Forests fall and lungs burn. What rescue remains?
Flood or drought, slaughter, contagion: *consummatum est*.
In the guilt of our comfort how can penance absolve us?
Switch channel, mute the sound. Search for beads and a missal.
For all the created, may your succour be felt in each heart.
That surplice-clad child of such certainty, where did he go?

Glory be to the Father, the Son and the Holy Spirit. Weep
with us, Lord, for how it is now, for how it will end. Amen.

# Night

Cirrus licks the moon. We drift as far, your fingers soft

as cloud, our nightly dark farewell. And then the dream.

*You're going to reap just what you sow.*
– Lou Reed (1942–2013)

# The Grievance

Arriving from elsewhere, a merchant grew wealthy
in the market at Izmir. Not without rivals, he soon
became known as The Democrat for the breadth of his produce:
mollusc and crab, clawed creatures from far-off salt water.
Though stories abounded as to his wives, their beauty and number

few claimed to have seen them, none could verify details.
Every night after closing his stall, people told, he'd vanish
down the maze of high alleys where no sun or moonlight
could penetrate, pass through a heavy locked door and into
a courtyard of fig trees and roses before entering the house.

Reports spread that on Mondays he'd call out 'Asifa?'
(who lived on her nerves), another day 'Fatima?' (whose eyes
were a lynx's on fire), on others to 'Mina?', 'Melika?',
'Cherifa?' – and how only silence replied. But when,
at the urging of mullahs, the police at last knocked

at his gate, none could explain how they found
not a trace, not their scent nor the qualities and faults
only he had ascribed to them; and never, deep as they dug,
the fine loam of ash and crushed bone that in tales
such as this always nurture such bountiful gardens.

# Escape

*Nature is a language, can't you read?* – Morrissey

Through school and college she was mocked, hostage to text
and cyber trolls, while to our shame we looked away. Not for years,
only at her strange and shocking end, did we learn how she'd
withdrawn, thrown out her phone and laptop, purged fridge
and cupboards of every processed packet, sugar-laden hit.

By night, it seems, she'd walk and jog the empty streets and parks
for hours, returning to a new regime of detox potions, blended berries,
pulses, nuts – convinced that in their purest state the juice and seeds
of pumpkin, sunflower, grapes, tomatoes; almond, anise, melon, peppers –
here was nature's path to energy and health, her hidden form, true self.

As weight fell from her, willowy at last, so thrilled was she at how
she felt, it's said she barely noticed as her nails took on a greenish tinge,
her hair grew daily bushier, more fibrous; that she accepted even when
from secret places, then ears and nose and lips, the first small shoots
emerged – growing only stronger when she cut them back.

Later, the autopsy revealed that certain seeds had fused, mutated:
found fertile ground and taken root. But once her disappearance
was reported and we joined the search, it wasn't for another week –
working through the copse beyond the bandstand – that someone
prodded at a tangle with their shooting-stick while another, just behind,

stared disbelieving as the bush appeared to bleed. Peering closer, he was first
to see the blank eyes staring back; the branches of her arms now raised
and rigid in a final stretch or prayer; her trunk and crown consumed
by tendrils, trailing vines. Bound, yet free at last. No longer subject to
our laws or imperfections. To which, in turmoil, we again bore witness.

# Shelter

*"I had it all. I had it all…"*
He rubs his eyes, wind-raw face —
each shadow, line and fold
another map, half-torn, erased —
these twenty, thirty journeys
spooling out, unravelling from
Gateshead, Oslo, California
but intersecting here, tonight,
this netherworld beneath
a nameless city — the hiss of rain
and traffic now the soundtrack
of their lives, the passing frames
of others flickering across the walls.
They've each descended: sodden, stinking,
bruised beyond repair or ruin —
night-guests in this hinterland,
transit passengers with, for now,
a pillow, warmth, the shelter
we all seek. *I had it all.*
The smile's just one more habit
he can't break. Cracked lips
parting on the gleam of bridgework,
LA's finest, like one last package
smuggled through. The mirror's
long rebuke. All that we have lost.

# Ecce Homo

Window-cleaner on his ladder,
reaching out one arm,                    the other.


Prisoner, naked, pegged out in the sun
honey-glazed for ant and bee                    to gorge on.


Bronzed Angel of the North embracing
Tyne and motorway –                    monumental, glowing.


Crossing lady walking out to plant her lollipop
assuming drivers see                    that traffic stops.


Preacher, eyes ablaze with fervour, hands aloft:
who are we all, spread-eagled,                    at a loss


if not God's shadows          making each our faithful cross?

# The Bridge

Above all else, the bridge must stand. Must bear
the traffic and the wind – their flow and stress
within its tensile span. And so the engineer
builds up his lines within a frame of gravity
and physics. Weighs extravagant aesthetics
with tolerance of corded steel. With bolts
and hawsers. Mud-sunk pilings deep as islands.
Then tarmac and cement to bind, which raise
the whole to sense and life – this string of quartz
across a darkened bay – from noun to verb, from
that to this – suspended here by luck or daring,
simply air. Humming, self-reliant now. Alive
with superstructure winds. Cars whipping by.

# The Ghost-Bike

Still and bitter night, our first week in this town
we hurry home along the towpath, huddled close

for warmth. Lamp-glow through the frosted branches,
cokey smoke of houseboats mingling with the vapour

on our breath, shawls of fog that hover on the oil-black water.
It's then we see it, glowing through the mist: a spectral sculpture

propped against a tree. Wreathed in hoary moss and riverweed,
snapped twigs now icicles amid its spokes, sheathed

utterly in ice. And as we pass we can't stop looking back,
as if, unprompted, we recognise our tangled pasts

have gathered there, have ossified behind us as we scurry on,
our first week in this town, laughing through the cold.

# Circadia

How easily we're lured from sleep – *nature's*
*soft nurse, the honey-heave dew of slumber.*
Before Edison's light-bulb moment zapped
our dark into history – spawned neon, the sickly
sodium chains of streets and motorways, smothered
out the stars – were we not subjects of the moon
and sun, content and hardy servants to their rhythms?

And now? In thrall to another Sky, to iPhones
Mp3s and instant messaging, sleep's become the enemy,
a fretful absence from our cravings: light and sound,
caffeine, booze, sequential fixes – the world no bigger
than a click, a button pressed, a finger-scrolling screen.

Edison himself considered sleep as *criminal*; Churchill,
Thatcher just *a waste of time.* And our other god,
crows Gordon Gecko, *never sleeps.* Thus our grasp
grows weak on this deep trance, Dekker's *golden chain*
*that holds together health and body*, our ebbing sanity.

# Sunflowers

Profligate helianthus,
arch
your promiscuous backs

a little further,
turn
those shameless eyes,

wanton seeds and buttery oil,
toward
your sky-bound suitor.

It must feel like
gazing
in a gilded mirror


at this source of
all
your heat and colour.

# Grace Notes

*for Joanna Dunham (1936–2014)*

Driving home from the service – the light, our eyes
the half-flooded roads, everything watery – even the radio
seems tuned in to you, Bruch's violin concerto
No.1, your favoured slow movement I'd so often catch
down the hall, years ago, as you worked in the studio:
head tilted, smock daubed with pigment, brush poised
baton-like at the canvas; or those fine Baroque trills
and flourishes that galvanised you – Scarlatti, Bach
'*luxuriant Vivaldi*' sailing from wide-open shutters
to the Montpeyroux garden where you painted, I wrote.
Not even a hurricane's worst (back from Morocco
thrilled by those Berber percussions, only to find
the barn flattened) could undo your poise, your beauty
your music. Years of favour and luck. Our grace notes.

# The Sigh

*(San Fernando, Trinidad)*

Then we called into the bank, First Citizens,
to change some traveller's cheques and
this was lunchtime, full of suited office-
workers, dirt-streaked road crew, pensioners
and shoppers – so the line was crazy, snaked
back and forth across the vaulted, marbled
vestibule, in and out of roped-off channels
back to where the doorman in his snazzy cap
just beamed and touched his brim and waved
more in until the air-conditioning said *no*,
just like the tellers, no more than two or three
who lounged at open windows while a multitude
of colleagues – guys in pressed white shirts,
sharp haircuts, women packed in pencil-skirts
and clicking heels – patrolled the desks and
yawning office-space we glimpsed beyond
the counter where a dozen windows more
were closed, watched them buzz themselves
with studied languor to and from the inner sanctum,
whatever files and vaults, excuses they could find
to save themselves from contact with a customer,
from apologies, advice or explanation, from
stepping out into a throng whose patience
now was fast evaporating in a hum of muttered
curses, shifting feet, gesticulation, threats –
we would have left to seek another branch
but feared a queue as long, so stayed while time
it seemed, slipped out instead to run its course
elsewhere – at least until, deep into a second hour,
our business done at last, we edged out through
the crowd and heard, close by the door, a thin
and stooped old man, face half-shadowed by
a dusty trilby, let out a sigh so long, so doleful –
a murmured 'Ah Lord' drawn-out beneath his breath –
it spoke for all of us: for forty, fifty people thrown
together to endure, for everything each day that
grates or riles or tests us to the edge, for life itself,
so that even now, years on and driven half-berserk

by automated menus, sales calls, parking zones,
our boss, our days, our nights, our weight of tasks,
ambitions unfulfilled...even now it's when those
same two words escape unbidden from our lips –
'Ah Lord' – that we remember and we honour him.

# Fires

Wars continue,
our planet smoulders on.

She hugs herself in the streetlight,
wonders where the stars have gone.

The lowlands go under,
columns trail through the dust;

even sand bleeds
in the after-burst.

Disease, famine, tempest –
winnowers all – do their worst,

rumour and envy
stoke the fire.

All we can embrace
is ourselves, these moments we own.

All we can leave
is love, which nothing can burn.

# The Egg

Fallen or pillaged, still somehow intact
it rests in my palm, a blue-speckled pebble
barely warm, feather-light.
                              Stooping, I peer

into laurel, leaves aquiver all spring
with the blackbirds' work, and it nestles again
in its twig-and-straw cup.
                              But later wonder:
was it kindness? There amid the clutch,
its unhatched companions, did my touch condemn?

Our world itself, according to Brahma, springs
from such a source. Hindu, Taoist, Greek –
even current cosmologists speak of the same
'cosmic egg'. Theologian or scientist
we flutter as much in the dark.
                              Had we but awe,
where is conflict? God is nature, nature God
and whatever our doctrine, we their betrayers.

Truth, if not answers, perhaps only
cosmonauts see. Our blue-speckled planet
feathered with cloud: brooding, sublime –
no more than a pebble in darkness,
an egg they might reach out
and cradle. To plunder or save.

## Legacy

No one will remember us,
not decades, millennia, even days
from now. Accepting is hard,
but our duty's to live.

                        Do you see
this pair of squirrels
playing high in the shadows –
not quite birds, not quite rats,
flying from branch to branch?

*Now you see me,*
*now you don't.*

## In the Aftermath

the land lay like a lake and where the land began

and the water did not was a riddle long drowned.

# Acknowledgements

Thanks are due to the editors of the following where some of these poems first appeared: *New Statesman, The Spectator, Sunday Herald, Aesthetica, Seam, Southlight, The Fenland Reed, Poem Magazine, Looking Up,* www.londonart.co.uk and *The Same* (USA).

Poems included in previous anthologies are 'Torrent' (*Snowdonia*, Seren 2018), 'Depth Charge' (*Herrings*: Poetry in Aldeburgh 2016), 'The Fabulists' (*Hand Luggage Only*), 'Sunburn' (*Only Connect*), 'Helvellyn' (*King's Lynn Silver Folio*) and 'The Bridge' (*Flirtation*: poems by The Joy of Six).

The following won competition prizes and several were included in related publications: 'The Grievance' (Wigtown/Scottish National), 'Jerusalem' (Peterloo), 'Heart' (Chapter One), 'Lost at Cadiz' and 'Ash' (Crabbe Memorial), 'Blood' (Yorkshire Open), 'Scrimshaw' (Robert Graves Prize), 'Passion' and 'Grace Notes' (Ver Poets).

'The Odds' was longlisted in the National Poetry Competition.

## About the author

André Mangeot has published two previous poetry collections, *Natural Causes* (Shoestring, 2003) and *Mixer* (Egg Box, 2005) along with two books of short stories, *A Little Javanese* (Salt, 2008) and *True North* (Salt, 2010) and has recently completed a novel. For over ten years he was a member of the poetry ensemble *The Joy of Six* which performed at many festivals across the UK. Alongside his writing he works in the charity sector and divides his time between Cambridge and South Wales.